The Success Guide

to

Teaching International Students

Online

Celeste Patton

Table of Contents

Chapter One
What is online teaching?

Have you ever thought about changing things up by stepping out of the classroom to online teaching? Do you want to stay home and earn money? If you answered yes to either of the two questions you should try online teaching. Educating students online is the new millennium way of teaching.

Online teaching is different in many ways from teaching in a traditional classroom. With online teaching, you as the teacher are providing a very interactive instruction to your student. The instruction will need to be more interactive than in the traditional classroom. You have to always remember that you are not actually sitting next to the student in the same room but rather face to face on a computer.

A high level of interaction is often needed to maintain your student's attention and to just keep things flowing in your classroom. Often a teacher may interact with the student by having special props related to the lesson. Having props and lesson materials helps the student to be able to better connect with what you are teaching. Examples of special props for a lesson in teaching about nouns could be: pictures of people, pictures of kid friendly toy places, pictures of familiar things the kids are able to identify.

With online teaching, the interaction must not be at a monotone voice level. Having a monotone voice will not keep the student active and interested. A great online teacher should have the following characteristics:

- Be happy! A student can sense if the teacher is not happy about the class or even seeing them. A happy teacher will create a happy friendly atmosphere for learning.

- Have special materials that allow the student to interact with the lesson. Special materials that allow students to draw on the computer screen with a stylus or finger if they are using an iPad. If appropriate for younger ages, a teacher may even have a microphone to help the child understand it is their turn to talk. Live interaction with the use of singing the learning material instead of just repeating the material can also help.

- You should make sure to remember to change their voice tone up a little bit. Throughout the lesson a way to keep things interesting for the student is by speaking in different voice pitches or tones. These things can be modified based on your student or students' age groups. A student of a younger age vs. a student of an older age will really appreciate the different teacher voice levels. A student of an older age may be comfortable with the monotone voice but each student is different.

- Ask higher order thinking questions throughout the lesson. Allow the student time to have input in the lesson and make comments throughout the teaching time. Asking questions during a lesson can help you as the teacher to see if the student comprehends what is being taught.

Online teaching can be done in multiple ways. As the educator you may instruct in the classroom by using a special classroom platform provided by the company you work for. A lot of the times a teacher may use skype, zoom or any type of online interface that allows you to interact with the student online.

Zoom is an online cloud platform that allows you to be able to have online interaction with someone by having conference or meetings. If needed, the download is free on the company website. If interested you may download the link for zoom at the following web address: https://www.zoom.us/Zoom is very simple to use, with very easy steps to follow once the link is downloaded for free. There are plans and pricing on the website for using zoom but the basic plan will be just fine to use for teaching online.

Skype is another online form of communication that is often used in online teaching. Skype allows you to have face-to-face classroom experiences, meetings and even voice calls if needed. If interested you may download the link for skype at the following web address: https://www.skype.com/en/

The online company may have even created their own classroom platform to use for teaching. Using the company's classroom platform often requires a little learning because they have special buttons and hidden things to enhance your teaching.

Usually the company you are working for will tell you the type of online interaction interface you will use for teaching your student or students.

You may be able to click and write on the computer screen with the computer mouse with some of these tools. Drawing on the computer screen with use of different color options when using the mouse can also be made possible. There may be buttons to press that make special sounds throughout the lesson. Often there will be objects in the classroom the student may be able to click and drag around the screen. There may also be interaction buttons on the online platform that enables the student to converse with the teacher.

What does an online teaching classroom look like?

Your classroom typically has student desk, chairs, white boards or chart boards and lots of other supplies for the students. But the look of an online classroom is very different.

1. ### Desk & Chair
   In an online classroom, you would have your personal teaching desk or teaching stand. Some teachers prefer to stand while teaching because it allows them to be more mobile with their movements. Standing while teaching helps you as the teacher to be able to do more physical activities and hand movements with you students while teaching, this is known as **Total Physical Response**[1]. If you choose to have a teaching desk then you should look into getting a chair that is very comfortable for the support of your body. It is very important to have a comfortable chair as you should remember you will

---

[1]Total Physical Response (TPR) is a language teaching method developed by James Asher, a professor emeritus of psychology at San José State University. It is based on the coordination of language and **physical** movement. ... The method is an example of the comprehension approach to language teaching. Wikipedia 2018

spend your entire time teaching sitting in the chair in front of a computer screen.

2. **Background**
   I highly recommend that your online classroom has a background behind your desk. There should be a background that is created of paper, poster or even a white board. If you use a white board as your background then you are able to have full use of it during class. You can use your whiteboard to write on during the lesson to post examples or even rewards you will be given to your student.

   A good background poster you could use should be something that is child-friendly that relates to the students you are teaching. If you are teaching online to students in another part of the world then I recommend using a poster background of a map. You could use the map in your classroom to introduce yourself, where you are from, and where your student is from compared to you. Whatever background you choose, just make sure that it is child-friendly and colorful. The colors on your background should not be very loud and vibrant because it may cause distractions to your students while teaching.

3. **Computer**
   You must be aware of the type of computer you are getting as well as the type of internet provider you are using. The type of computer you are getting matters because some computers may not have certain capabilities needed when deciding which company to work for. The computer speed is a major concern. You should be aware of the internet provider as well as how fast your computer is processing while in use. Often companies that you work for online will require you to not use your Wi-Fi but instead to hard wire your computer to the wall. Hard wiring your computer to the wall is simply just making sure you have the modem and electrical socket in your classroom. You are basically plugging your internet connection into the wall directly from your computer.

   After you have your computer and internet connection, you are able to put your computer onto your desk. The best way to prop your computer on your desk is by using a computer prop stand. They are fairly inexpensive but rather useful for the health of your hands and wrist. It is very important that you make sure your computer is set on your desk at a certain angle that allows you to not have to look down at your student. Before teaching you should make sure to adjust your monitor that allows for your head to be in a comfortable upright position.

4. *Camera*

   If you are working online as an educator, you will need a computer with some kind of camera. Having a camera is very essential to your career as an online teacher. Often, people purchase computers with built-in cameras. A built-in camera is useful because you do not have to turn the camera on and off with a switch or even make sure it is plugged up. All you have to do is turn your computer on and most of the time your camera is ready to go. Sometimes, you may run into a technical issue that does not allow the computer to turn on but that is something that cannot be prevented. Another option is to have an external camera if you don't have a built-in camera. An external webcam can help to provide better image quality and clearer audio for teleconferencing and sharing live information.

5. *Computer mouse*

   A computer mouse is something that is useful to have while teaching. Laptops come with a touchpad that is easy to use for navigating around the computer screen. But an external mouse is better to use when teaching online. By using an external mouse you are able to easily make drawings and writings on the computer screen. External mice are fairly cheap and can be found at the neighborhood computer stores or stores carrying materials for computers.

6. *Headphones*

   Headphones are very much needed when working online as a teacher. You should make sure to wear headphones that have the capabilities of canceling out background noises. Headphones that have the extended microphone are commonly used throughout online teaching. There are some people that use basic ear buds with the small microphone that is located on the cord. If you choose to use the ear buds vs. the headset, just remember the headset will cancel out the background noise and are more stable on your head. With the headset you are able to move around more with the extended microphone not going anywhere. The ear buds may give you a problem of falling out of your ears if not placed in properly. The ear buds with the microphone on the cord may sometimes shift around as you move. This makes it hard for your students to hear you through the speaker.

7. *Lighting*
Lighting is another key component of having an effective online classroom environment. You will need to make sure to have the appropriate lighting in the room you are using as your classroom. You will need to make sure to switch on your light in the room as well as some kind of lamp. Using the regular light fixture in your room is usually not enough lighting for having a well-lit classroom. A floor lamp or a desk lamp that is near the computer that is being used to teach in the online classroom is very beneficial. Some people even use small computer lights that clip to the computer and light up the screen. Extra lighting is needed to help make sure your student can see you in a bright well-lit classroom.

8. *DIGITAL LESSON*
When in the classroom, you will not need to get your teacher lesson plan book or curriculum notes. Rather the curriculum content will be online for you to use. The lesson needed to be taught is usually an easy download link to click while you are in the classroom. The classroom content is a digital lesson that will be used to teach the student.

What my personal classroom looks like

My online classroom is located in the far back upstairs in my home. I chose to have the classroom as far back in the house as I can to help eliminate noise and use my Logitech headphones during class time to help cancel out background noise while I teach. I am a stay-at-home mom with two kids and a puppy that love to create exciting noise.

Often, during my class time my children are asleep and when they awaken, my husband is around to help maintain a quiet classroom. I have my desk set up in a corner that is to the back of the room near the side of the window.

The window helps to give me natural lighting in the classroom while teaching. I make sure to keep on the standard size light fixture in the room as well as a lamp. The type of lamp I use is a small desk lamp that I project towards my face onto the background. The direction of the lighting helps to brighten up my face and background as I teach.

I use a standard size chair that is firm but at the same time soft seating for my body. Right behind my chair is my whiteboard that I have secured into the wall. Personally, I love using a white board in the classroom as my background. Using a background in the classroom has helped me to make sure I keep the classroom active, so I am able to have a fully functional classroom as well as an active classroom to teach in.

For teaching online, I use a standard sized laptop to interact with my students as an educator. The laptop I use has a built-in web camera that I am able to view the students with. I do use a personal computer mouse to help easily maneuver around the screen. Often the touch pads of the laptop are a little more difficult to use while teaching.

As far as the internet connection, I use the Wi-Fi signal that I have throughout my home. Online teaching companies do recommended to plug your computer directly into the router rather than to use Wi-Fi. It is said that plugging your computer directly into the router will help to have a stronger connection speed for your live class. A trick that I have learned to do is to have a backup internet connection available whenever there is a problem. For my backup internet connection I use my cell phone's hotspot. Just about all cell phone companies offer the service for you at a low monthly price. I pay $10 a month to have a

mobile hotspot [2] available whenever I need it. If my connection is really slow while teaching using Wi-Fi, I am able to quickly turn on my mobile hotspot to continue.

[2]A mobile hotspot is an ad hoc wireless access point that is created by a dedicated hardware device or a smartphone feature that shares the phone's cellular data. Mobile hotspots are also known as portable hotspots. ... Another option is using a smartphone to connect other devices. Copyright 1999 - 2018, TechTarget

Chapter 2
What are the pros of online teaching?

Teaching online is a great alternative to teaching in a public or private classroom outside of your home. There are many pros for teaching online that you should take into consideration when deciding if this job is for you.

1. Independence
   One of the most appealing features of teaching online is the opportunity to be an independent worker. Having a virtual job allows you to not be concerned about waking up to go to a place of work outside of your home. Instead, your independence will allow you to work where ever you may be. You will have the opportunity to work inside of your home or even work on the road while you travel. Your independence gives you the freedom to work in another part of the world as long as you have your computer and internet connection with you.

2. Family time
   Now you will have the flexibility to be able to spend quality time with your family. Working online allows you to not have to miss those special games your kids have. You no longer have to miss special events or places to go with your family. Your amount of family time will improve drastically. You will have more time to see your kids grow and be able to be that great mom or dad that you want to be.

3. Savings
   You no longer will have to spend money on your work clothes. Often, people working online do not purchase multiple outfits for teaching. Instead one of the easiest things to do is to rotate around a few of your favorite online teaching outfits. Say good bye to having to purchase loads of classroom material that your students need to succeed. No need to pay for the school programs. As a teacher, everyone is highly recommended to participate in. Can you imagine how much money you would

save? Not to mention saving extra money on daycare expenses. If you have children being able to save on daycare is a huge deposit back into your account.

4. No lesson plan writing
    Usually all lessons needed to teach online are provided for you. This may be different if a company is paying you a additional fee to come up with your own creative plans. That means no afterschool team meetings. No taking time out of your lunch time to plan for the next school week or 2 weeks. What a stress reliever this has been for me.

5. Free time
    As a virtual teacher you no longer have to maneuver your doctor appointments around your work schedule. You have the freedom to choose the days and times you want to work. You will create your own schedule vs. having to work every day. If you choose to take a day off all you will have to do is not open your schedule up for the day. You may do this only if the company you are working for do not have requirements for specific times and days you must work. The company I work for located in China allows me to create my own schedule based upon my own needs.

Chapter 3
The Cons of Teaching Online

Becoming a virtual teacher is great but there are a few cons to teaching online to make sure to consider before choosing this as your career. Here are a few:

1. No insurance benefits
    A major concern with teaching online is having insurance benefits. Working as a public or private school teacher, you are given a choice of full benefits. In most online companies such as the ones working online from a foreign company, do not offer you insurance. If you do not have a spouse that has medical insurance then you will need get a private medical insurance on your own.

2. No TRS
    The teacher retirement system is not offered in teaching online for companies that hire foreigners. So as an educator you will have to make sure to save up for your retirement for your later years.

3. Early work hours
    If working in a foreign company such as China, you will undergo the concern of what hours to work. The different time zone that students are in around the world affects your schedule.

    For example: If working in China online, the students tend to go to school during the evening hours in the USA. So what that means is the United States working hours will be very early in the mornings. Your mornings may start at 4am or earlier.

4. Hard to form student to teacher relationship
    The online classroom is a much different space used for learning than a public classroom. It is harder for a teacher to form that student to teacher relationship of trust and understanding as the teacher. Often times you will not see the student you are teaching frequent enough to develop a

teacher/student bond with them. If working for a foreign company often the companies are rather large and allow the students to pick their own teachers to work with or try out.

Chapter 4
Counting the Costs of Online Teaching

As a teacher you often have to spend a lot of your money to prepare your classroom with extra school supplies, decorations and personal items for yourself. As an online teacher, you will not need to spend a lot of money on your classroom. The majority of online educators work from the comfort of their home so spending money on a classroom of 22 is not needed. Most of the things purchased for teaching online are not needed at the expensive teacher stores. You really could create or purchase your supplies from local stores.

One of my favorite stores to purchase items for my online classroom is the dollar store. Purchasing items at a dollar store or any store is inexpensive and will save you lots of money. Often, teachers go to the big well-known teacher stores without first looking at the small expensive stores such as the Dollar Store, Dollar Tree, Family Dollar, Dollar General even the $1 target area. You have to remember that the things you purchase will be used by you and not 22 students so the amount you need will be small. Just a few examples of products and cost of items I have used in my online classroom are listed below:

1. Cookie Boards: You can use these boards to put magnetic letters on or any type of object that is made of magnets. Cost is about 1-2 dollars.
2. Hand-held White Board: A white board you can hold in your hand will help you to be able to write things down quickly so you will be able to show the student. Cost is about 3-5 dollars.
3. Magnetic Letters: If you are teaching younger students' magnetic letters are very important in helping you to not just say words but to identify letters in words. Cost is about 3-5 dollars.
4. Dry erase markers: Markers that you are able to dry erase with are great in online teaching. You can have the markers handy for quick writing and showing students information you are writing. Cost 2-3 dollars.

5. Magic Erasers: Before looking at the dollar store I would use the Mr. Clean magic eraser. But the dollar store magic erasers in the cleaning area work just as well. Cost 1-2 dollars.

6. Stickers: You can get stickers for just about any occasions for boys and girls. Younger kids love the stickers, especially stickers with their favorite characters on them. Cost about 1-3 dollars.

7. Mini Rewards for students: With teaching being online it is very important to try and have engaging rewards for them. I like to purchase small magnetic games they can win if doing a good job. Cost is about 3-5 dollars.

If you have a creative mind you are even able to save money and make your own things needed for your classroom. This in return saves you even more money because you are only making one of those items. I often make classroom items and laminate them after I create. If you enjoy being creative, it is best if you purchase a small laminator from your store of choice. A small laminator may cost you around $25-$35. Having a small laminator will save you lots of time in the long run of your online teaching career.

Chapter 5
Organizations Needing Online Teachers

When deciding to change from working outside of your home to online teaching, there may be some concerns. The major concern that people run into is finding a job that is legit.

In other words, a legit job is a job that you will get paid from and that is actually real. There are so many work from home jobs that are false advertisement. It took me 5 months to find the online teaching company I currently work for. Most educational companies that are not in the United States are looking for Native English speakers with qualifications of an **ESL teacher**[3].

The following list is of Chinese Companies that offer remote teaching jobs for ESL teachers. This is a list that will help you to get started on looking for your online teaching job. You may ask, "Are there more companies available?" The answer is yes. Again, this is just a start of companies for you to look into working for. Each company that I will list has their own special requirements to be considered as a teaching candidate. The following list is not all the companies I have applied to or interviewed with, but this is just a comprehensive list to help you with your online teaching choice.

The following are the names & websites you can check out when you want to apply for your online teaching position in China.

1. **Magic Ears:** https://t.mmears.com/

2. **Sprout4Future:** http://teacher.rouchi.com/#/employ/create

3. **VIPKID:** http://vipkidteachers.com/

4. **TEOtutur:** https://teotutor.com/jobs/

5. **Liulishou:** https://www.liulishuo.com/en/index.html

---

[3] English as a second language (ESL) teachers instruct students whose first language isn't English, in reading, writing and conversing effectively. These professionals are also sometimes called English for speakers of other languages (ESOL) teachers. **Study.com 2018**

6. **PK Fish:** https://t.pipi100.com/

7. **EtalkABC:** http://www.etalkabc.com/

8. **USKid:** https://teacher.uskid.com/

9. **KK Talkee:** http://t.kktalkee.com/

10. **Waijaoyi:** http://www.waijiaoyi.com/esl/

11. **UUABC:** https://www.uuabc.com/

12. **51talk:** http://www.51talk.ph/phweb/page/index/

13. **Palfish:** https://www.ipalfish.com/teacher/

14. **BlingAbc:** https://www.blingabc.com/

15. **Koolearn:**
    http://winning.koolearn.com/kouyu/?form=index

16. **Panda/ ABC:** https://www.teachfuture.com/

17. **BiteABC:** http://www.biteabc.com/Teacher/recruit/

18. **Acadsoc:** http://tutor.acadsoc.ph/

19. **SayABC:** http://t.sayabc.com/

20. **98Kids:** http://www.98kid.com/

21. **HiTutor:** http://www.hitutorhr.com/browse_job.php

22. **HelloKid:** http://tutor.hellokid.com/

23. **Wonderkids:** http://www.wonderkidsenglish.com/

24. **Landi:** https://teacher.landi.com/

25. **First Future:**
    http://www.firstfuturejobs.com/contact/index.html

26. **ABC 360:** http://www.abc360.com/

27. **NiceKid:** http://www.nicekid.com/

28. **QuQuABC:** http://www.sojump.hk/jq/8412738.aspx

29. **Talk915:** http://www.talk915tutor.com/

30. **Boxfish:** https://www.boxfish.cn/

31. **Huijang:** https://www.hujiang.com/

32. **DaDaABC:**
   https://www.dadaabc.com/teacher/resumewrite

33. **AL07:** https://tutor.alo7.com/

When applying for companies in China please note that sometimes their websites are not always translated into English. You may need to translate the website into English by simply clicking on a button on your computer. Click anywhere on the website you are on and select translate to whatever language you desire.

The list I have provided for you is a very short list of online Chinese companies that you can apply to. There are 100s of other companies that you may look into finding an online job. It is very possible to find online teaching jobs in North American Companies, British Companies, Russian Companies, Spanish Companies, European Companies, Japanese and even Korean Companies.

Chapter 6
How to Become an Online Teacher

Usually companies in China are looking for teachers with a Bachelor's degree and who also are Native American speakers. Please keep in mind that the classroom size will range based upon the company you choose. Sometimes you will have a classroom of 1 to 4 students to teach. The classroom ages will range from elementary to early middle school ages. Some students will come to you already knowing English but most students will come to you in need of learning English as well as you teaching them. Most companies hire teachers with the desire of the Native American teacher teaching the United States Curriculum as well as having ESL skills.

Often you are looked at as more of the perfect candidate if you have an ESL certification or a **TESOL certification**[4].

A good place to obtain a TESOL Certification is from groupon. On **groupon**[5] you are able to take an online class with learning modules that will train you on what TESOL is. The online class will consist of reading and quizzes. The website for groupon is https://www.groupon.com/. If you are currently a teacher coming from a private or a public school you may already have an ESL (English as Second Language) certification that you earned through a series of teaching courses. This certification just says you are able to teach students that have English as their second language.

Having a great resume that is formatted well and easy to read is something else that is looked for in an online teacher. It will definitely help you out as a teaching candidate to have a great online educator

[4] TESOL Teaching English to speakers of other languages (TESOL) is the preferred certification for teaching ESL in U.S. public schools. This pedagogy is designed for teaching students from any number of different backgrounds who live in an English-speaking country, but who learned another language at birth.   **2018 USC Rossier School of Education**

[5] Groupon is an American worldwide e-commerce marketplace connecting subscribers with local merchants by offering activities, travel, goods and services in 15 countries. **2018 Wikipedia**

resume. Your resume that you currently use for getting jobs is ok but it can be better if you add a few things to it. You should make sure your resume shows the following:

1. How you have been able to work with diverse students.
2. Your education background as a teacher
3. Online or smaller classroom teaching ability
4. Your teaching management skills with difficult students or all students (Teaching Style)
5. Tell that you are a Native American Teacher (very important)

Please refer to the sample resume template that is within this book as to how to easily list these different details in your online teaching resume. There are many ways to write a resume, this is just a sample template to help get you started.

Your Name

Native American Teacher

State/USA

OBJECTIVE:

What are you seeking? Who are you? How will you be helpful or beneficial to the company?

Highlights about yourself as an educator

1. I am a responsible teacher.
2. Have great time management skills.
3. Highlight 3

PROFESSIONAL EXPERIENCE

Employment 1: Talk about briefly what your most recent job was and your professional responsibilities. Should be no more than 3 sentences. A long resume takes the employer to long to read and they get dis-interested.

Employment 2: Talk about briefly what your job was and your professional responsibilities.

Employment 3: Talk about briefly what your job was and your professional responsibilities.

EDUCATION:

This is where you list your Education level. Your degrees and types of certifications you have. If you do not have an ESL or TESOL certification you should say you are in the process of getting one. Make sure to obtain the ESL or TESOL certification quickly while you are in the process of looking for an online international teaching job.

Chapter 7
What does the online teaching interview look like?

Interviewing for an online teaching position is a little bit different from interviewing for a job that is outside of your home. An educator that works in a public or private school will usually have a face-to-face interview that will allow you to sit and talk with the interviewer. You are able to sometimes walk around and explore your place of work. You are even able to use body language as well as physical touch (such as shaking hands and handing over your resume) with the interviewer.

A working from home interview may look a lot different than the normal interview. The work from home interview will look like the following:

- You are in front of a computer for your interview.
- You will have to make sure to a well-lit room for accurate use of your camera, maybe you will need to have the room light on along with a few lamps.
- You will need to dress professional from the waist up if you are sitting. If you are standing it is wise that you wear a full set of professional clothing attire.
- You will need to use more body language to show your expressions and interest when talking and in conversation.
- Make sure to have good posture when you are sitting.
- Be sure you have a great background wherever you decide to do your interview at. A background that is not to distracting or full of noise.
- Most importantly making sure you smile a lot and have a positive attitude.

Your facial expressions and body movements are strongly watched when you are interviewing over the computer.

As a current online teacher I can remember what my interview looked like. I made sure to be a fully-dressed professional because I was not sure if I was going to need to stand or just sit. The interviewer may have asked me to demonstrate something that required me to stand. I did my interview in a bedroom in the back of my house away from the family and barking dog. I even-wore headphones to help eliminate the background noises I may have. I sat in a very comfortable chair with back support that forced me to sit in an up- right position. Since I was interviewing for an online teaching class I made sure to have things in my background that pertained to education and teaching and the colors were very bright. I used a few borders in the background to help appear as if I was in the classroom along with writing my name on a whiteboard. My whiteboard was in my background with the border around it and my name on it with puppets, letters, and numbers hanging around it. Since I knew the company I was interviewing for, I even put their name on the whiteboard behind me.

What kinds of interview questions will they ask me?

The type of interview questions that will be asked depends on the company that you are looking to get the online job from. But a few common questions that are often asked are listed below.

1. Where did you hear about this company from?
2. Have you ever taught an online class before?
3. How would you manage your teaching time if you have a problem during the lesson?
4. How do you use body movements to interact with the class?
5. Can you read this lesson page 1 and 2 and ask as if I am a student, how would you teach me?
6. How do you handle a child that does not want to cooperate during class?
7. What would you do if a student finishes the class too early?
8. Do you feel as if you should be able to communicate with the parent about issues in the classroom?
9. Can you tell me about a time you taught an ESL student, what strategies did you use with him or her to understand the lesson?
10. Are you comfortable with last minute classes that are scheduled?
11. How would you keep a class engaging online?

12. What would you do if you had a computer problem and couldn't teach the class? Do you have a alternate computer or internet connection?

13. What type of internet connection and computer do you have? Your internet speed?

14. How would you introduce yourself to a student in the classroom? Can you demonstrate?

15. Are you willing to provide a class demo of teaching the entire lesson to an actual student that we give you as a test class? This will show them how you interact with the students and how you are able to complete the lesson in the desired time allowed by the company.

16. Can you provide a class demo to us of you teaching the lesson we will provide to you? The lesson is usually given to you before the interview takes place and the interviewer will tell you if you passed or not based upon the demo lesson you do. With the demo lesson you will ask as if you have a kid in front of you and teach the lesson. You may have a choice to do the demo lesson with an interviewer. Whichever one feels more comfortable to you is what you should choose.

Most interview questions are usually pretty easy and straight-forward. There are usually not any thought-provoking questions that you will have to answer. Sometimes an interviewer will just give you a scenario in the form of a question and how you respond to that scenario will answer most of the questions for them.

Chapter 8
Parental expectations

Expectations of parents from an online teacher can vary. Just like with a public school job as a educator, you will have parents that expect you to go above and beyond for their child and some that care less. With online classes, most parents that I have met in the classroom or have left me feedback have been very involved with the learning of their child. Keep in mind that most parents have to pay for the online English speaking classes, so they do not want to waste their money on a teacher that is not meeting their expectations for their child or for them as the parent.

1   **Your professional appearance**
    You should always open your camera with a professional look. Just because you do not have to leave your house does not mean you should keep your pajamas on. When a student opens their computer in time for class with you they should see a professional-looking teacher. You should have your hair nicely done or pulled back so the student is able to see your face. Even if you are only seeing children in front of the screen, do not think that the parent is not watching from the side or watching the playback of the class. These parents want their child to have the experience of their child feeling like they are in an actual classroom. So, in your background while on your computer, make sure you do not have clutter or clothes thrown around. Your surrounding will greatly affect the way you appear as a professional educator. Most companies ask that you look professional by wearing a certain color. The color is usually a symbol that the parents are able to associate with the teacher working for the company. It is always nice to dress up whatever you are wearing by having a simple blazer to put over your shirt. You could even go as far as wearing a very nice necklace to dress up you attire. For women makeup is a big plus. Makeup can make the skin glow and you appear very bright and fresh while teaching class. Don't forget that lipstick! A nice bold lipstick (not neon colors) will help your lips to pop out for the student. When talking the student will often pay close attention to your lips. Overall, parents are looking for a nice clean look from you as the

professional. No one wants their teacher to look like they don't care or just rolled out of bed.

2 Your professional attitude

Your professional attitude means a lot to parents no matter what company you work for. You should always come to class with a bright smile and ready to teach. Come to class being ready to teach and excited to see your student. Perhaps you did not want to see a certain student today because of their last classroom behavior but just remember that the class will only last for a short period of time. That alone should be enough to make you smile. Just set to the side, feelings you may have about a student for whatever the reasons may be and have them enjoy learning the lesson. Your professional attitude she always remain positive with full of smiles.

Chapter 9
Interacting with students and parents

It is very important to have interaction between you and the student in your online classroom. As a teacher, you have to remember that when a student opens their camera they should feel as if they are inside of a classroom. A student should open their camera to a smiling face from a teacher that is ready to teach. You should create a positive online classroom atmosphere for you and your student. If you are an online educator for students in China or any other foreign company, the student-to-teacher interactions can be similar.

1. One way to make sure you have good interactions with the student is by having a conversation with them. You can simply ask them their name and tell them yours in a friendly way. You can ask the student their age and what they did in school today. You could even tell them what you did for the day. Often, before class if you are able to read a little information about a student, it will sometimes help you to interact better. You are opening up the classroom with the atmosphere of interaction using communication. This also helps to relax the mood of the classroom.

2. Get creative on different ways to use your whiteboard. Often, teachers use a hand-held white board or a white board that is hung behind them in the classroom. You can make your whiteboard interactive by having magnetic letters or numbers. With your whiteboard you could use the letters to create words or phrases that you want your student to learn.

3. Use communication all throughout the class lesson. You can easily make a class more engaging full of interaction by extending the lesson topic. In what you are teaching, you may choose to interact with the student more by asking more questions or having them speak on how they relate to the lesson. This is a student-to-teacher interaction that forces the student to use their higher order thinking skills to communicate.

4. Make the learning fun. A student often learns more when they feel as if the learning is interesting and they are having fun. You can make learning fun by having an online interaction through playing learning games. The learning games should always relate to your lesson and should be something quick.

5. If a parent is visible in the classroom, the interaction you have should be brief and pleasant. Feel free to greet the parent by saying "hello" and "how are you?" A parent is looking for a teacher that is able to speak well and have a positive interaction with their child. The parent is expecting you to keep their child interested in the lesson as well as challenging for the student. Sometimes they are expecting the interaction to be engaging enough to keep the child from acting out in the classroom.

The online company I work for is located in China and the parents want a lot of interaction among the teacher and their child. If I am teaching a young student of maybe 5 years old, the parents are usually around. So the teacher-to-student and teacher-to-parent interaction takes place immediately.

Since time for teaching is limited I usually just say hi to the parent and tell them my name. The parent most often does not know English but is able to comprehend what is being said by my actions. Sometimes, I have a parent of a student near them in the classroom and I try to speak to them, and often they are able to actively communicate with me and tell me a little bit about their child. They are able to tell me what they would like to make sure I work on for the day when teaching the targeted lesson. After speaking to the parent I interact with the student by smiling and introducing myself as their teacher. I even ask the student their age while at the same time correcting their language abilities. This brief active interaction with the student and parent may take me up to 2-3 minutes before the lesson. When the lesson starts to take place during the scheduled class time, the classroom remains fully active and engaging for the student. For younger students, the active engagement I sometimes use when singing songs is a play microphone. When I am singing or wanting the student to speak, I simply put the microphone up to my mouth and then move it up to their mouth. This interaction also helps the student to know that it is their turn to speak. Throughout the lesson, whenever I want the student to practice writing a learned vocabulary word or a simple sentence, I use an interaction tool. I interact with the student by using a large oversized pen or pencil that most of the time they laugh when they see it, to allow them to know I want them to write.

The computer screen that you are teaching on is a very fun interactive tool to use between you and the student. While teaching, you can use the screen to have the student draw, circle or underline things on the computer. This only works if the company you are working for has the lesson in a format that allows you to write on the computer screen. My interactions with the student is often full of energy that allow us to have fun with the lesson. If I have an older student that I am teaching, the energy level I may have is not so high because they often are not wanting to interact at that level.

With older students we usually interact by speaking on how we relate to the lesson and giving examples of different things we are learning about. With younger students, often the energy level has to be high to keep their attention so we often interact with each other by using puppets or teddy bears. The younger students love using puppets for interacting with the teacher because they are able to get out their own favorite stuffed animals and have a little fun with them all while learning. As the classroom lesson comes to an end I use high fives and online handshake interactions to help them know they had a great day in class.

Chapter 10
Getting Bookings and Providing Feedback about student

Ok, so you have signed your contract and bought all your things needed for teaching your first class! Now how do you get those students in your classroom? Different companies have different ways of having you start teaching. There are some companies that may have a set schedule for you to follow. A computer may generate a schedule for you. This schedule will include the times, student's names, and what you will be teaching them.

You may even be a teacher for a company that you only teach certain students that they will email you about throughout your teaching with the company. The more common way most teachers begin teaching their first student is through bookings. Bookings are when a parent is able to see your schedule and they are able to select which date on your schedule will be a great time for their child to take classes. Often, you will have to set your schedule in advance for parents or for your staff members at your company to see so that you are selected to teach a certain class with a student.

At the company I work for before you get hired you have to create a profile where you will briefly say something about yourself (introduction) while in your classroom. This introduction is something that parents will be able to view before selecting you to be their child's teacher. As a teacher, I often set my schedule about 4 weeks in advance so that I am available and parents are able to book. My schedule is very consistent; it does not change from week to week. You have to remember that a parent is looking at your schedule to have consistent time schedules throughout the week for their child. It is best that a student has a few consistent classes with you as their teacher. It happens very often that my schedule will get booked very quickly with other students if parents do not book ahead of time. So, sometimes parents may request that you open a special classroom time for them if it is not on your schedule. Often, in some companies, your schedule is set in stone starting at the beginning of the week. What I mean is that at the beginning of the week if you have 6 classes for throughout the week then that is it for you.

The company I am with have something called booking frenzy. This is simply just a time when parents are able to book you before your classroom booking schedule gets filled up with students. This booking frenzy is very useful for teachers that have established a reputation among the parents and students and are well-known, so your teaching is desired. Most teachers will not get their schedule completed filled by the booking frenzy that is held during the company's scheduled time. So throughout the week, parents are still able to book classes with you up till the day of the teaching. I often have parents that book a class with me up to 1 hour before the scheduled time to start the class. Booking right before the start time of class is called a short notice booking class. The company I am at pays the teachers extra money for having a short notice class to teach. With parents having control of booking the classes for their child, it is likely that not all your classes may (or may not) get filled. There are often a lot of teachers that are in the company as an online teacher. So with that being said, you are pretty much competing for popularity among the parents and students to get booked. This does not necessarily mean that you will never get a class because a parent will not book you. With this company I am at they have classes that allow students to trial out the company to see if they like it. So the trial classes that some students will take are most of the time given to newer teachers that have not had classes that need to get their schedule filled with bookings.

Writing effective feedback about the student after class

Once the class is over and you have taught your student, you will often have to write feedback. The feedback will usually need to be very brief and straight to the point. In some companies, you write the feedback to the parent and the feedback to another teacher. So the feedback that you will write to the parent will be only about what the student did in class for the day. You should include the following things in your feedback to parents:

1. How you enjoyed class with their child for the day.
2. The student's behavior in class.
3. What the child learned for the day.

4. Things that the child did well in class on.
5. Something in class that the parent can continue to work with their child at home on. Make sure this comment is not made in a negative manner.
6. Include new vocabulary words, sight words, sentences, examples of what you would want the parent to work on with their child. If the child is old enough it may be them reading the feedback on their own without parent support.

Teacher to teacher feedback may have the following details:

1. What you had to do if anything to keep the students attention and maintain behavior while in the classroom.
2. What the student did well at.
3. What the student should continue to work on in the next class.

Feedback about the student's class may be in a different format for each company, but this is just an example of different things you should say in your classroom feedback. What you write in the parent feedback is very important because usually this is your only form of communication to the parent.

I must say that if you are working for a company that is not in the United States it is very often that the parents will have to translate. Parents will often need to translate your feedback into their own language to see what you have written. So it is wise to make sure you stay away from words that are very descriptive but rather stay straight to the point because when translating words start to become confusing.

It is very often words will be translated to say something you may not have meant to say when parents are translating into their own language. You may feel comfortable with writing out your feedback to the parent and then inserting it into an online translator to view how your information may translate. When using the translator online you will need to be able to know the language that the parent speaks in order to select the correct translate button.

Chapter 11
Tax Write-Offs

After a great year of working as an online teacher, you have to make sure you are prepared for filing taxes. Most online teaching companies will request as part of the application process that you submit a W-9 form. The W-9 form will be given to you by the company you are working for. So when tax season comes around the company will issue out to you a 1099 MISC form with your work compensation that you have made as a contractor with the company.

It is your option to set money aside for paying taxes at the end of the year or pay them quarterly. What you should do is to make sure you keep absolutely everything you purchase that has anything to do with your job as an online teacher. Anything that you spend money on to keep your job actively going is a receipt needed to be kept for auditing purposes for taxes. There are an overwhelming amount of tax write offs that you are able to qualify for as an online educator. As an online educator you generally work as a contractor, you are self-employed.

Business Write Offs could be the following for you

1   Business startup cost:
    What did it take to get your online teaching ready to start up and going. What materials did you have to purchase? Some examples could be the following:

    - Desk

    - Lamp

    - Desk

    - Computer

    - White board

    - Office chair

2   Communication write-offs that you may write off for your taxes are listed below

    - Cell phone use for hotspot when your internet is not working

- Cell phone service you use to receive messages or the app to communicate
- Internet service provider you have to use to have that online teaching platform Your cell phone monthly billing payments
- Health insurance premiums can be deducted if you are self employed

3 Meals and entertainment you may have had with colleagues discussing the company youwork for are deductions you may take off your taxes.

4 Supplies you may need to help maintain the class are tax write offs. Supplies such as:

- pens
- paper
- pencils
- pads
- copy paper
- printer ink
- toner
- calendars
- planners
- marker
- tape
- ruler
- pencil box
- storage box
- white board

5 Home office expenses are major tax write-offs that a lot of people often forget about. Your home office space should be exclusively used for your online business.

- The office space length by width will be needed so that you can deduct the office space

- You may deduct a portion of the amount you pay in mortgage interest for your home

- The actual mortgage interest amount deducted will be based upon the room size that you use as your business (online classroom). You will need to have proof of your interest paid on your mortgage by using your end of the year tax statement provided by your mortgage lender or lenders.

6   Utilities are another major write off that is often forgotten by many when it comes to tax write offs. The amount you pay for utilities will be a deduction that is able to be written off as a deduction. The amount of the deduction will be dependent upon the size of your room for your business. If you are working with a tax professional they will calculate the amount you use on utilities from your bill. The utility tax amount will be based upon a percentage used by your room size. Utility deductions are: household gas, water, even the amount you pay for trash pickup.

7   Repair expenses you make on your home are also deductions that can be made to your taxes. The amount of the deduction will be dependent upon the size of your room for your business. If you are working with a tax professional, they will calculate the amount you use on repair expenses. Make sure to have receipts!! Repairs and maintenance expenses are related to your entire home. Examples include: painting the house, roof repairs, gutter cleaning, etc.

8   Insurance expenses you paid on your home are tax deductions you may write off. All homes have home owners insurance. The amount you pay to keep insurance on your home is a great tax deduction. The amount of the deduction will be dependent upon the size of your room for your business. If you are working with a tax professional they will calculate the amount you paid on home owners insurance for your room.

9   Your home association fees you pay in your neighborhood for the end of the year can be deducted on your taxes as well. The amount of the deduction will be dependent upon the size of your room for your business. If you are working with a tax professional they will

calculate the amount you paid on home association fees for your room.

Conclusion

Teaching online is a great opportunity. Deciding to teach online is a great choice to have as an educator. Teaching online gives you the freedom to choose your schedule and job work load. You even get a chance to save on your taxes with teaching online. So have you ever thought about changing things up by stepping out of the classroom to online teaching? Do you want to stay home and earn money? If you answered yes to either of the two questions you should try online teaching. Educating students online is the new millennium way of teaching.

94496112R00024

Made in the USA
Lexington, KY
30 July 2018